CONTENTS

▲ *Castle Howard, Yorkshire.*

IMPORTANT DATES

1901 Queen Victoria dies, Edward VII becomes King

1906 Britain launches the first 'dreadnought' battleship

1908 New Territorial Force is formed

1910 Edward VII dies, George V becomes King

1911 The last national census in Britain before the war

28 June 1914 The shooting of Austrian Archduke Francis Ferdinand

26 July 1914 Austria declares war on Serbia

1 August 1914 Germany declares war on Russia

3 August 1914 Germany declares war on France

4 August 1914 Germany invades Belgium, Britain declares war on Germany

22–24 August 1914 Battle of Mons, followed by battle of Ypres in October/November

1914 All Britain's coal mines are nationalised (until 1921)

April 1915 Second battle of Ypres, first gas attack on the Western Front

25 April 1915 Start of Gallipoli campaign

23 May 1915 Italy joins the Allies (Britain, France, Russia)

31 May 1915 First German air raids on London

12 October 1915 Shooting of Edith Cavell by Germans causes outrage

February 1916 Conscription of single men aged 18–41, thousands of women join the workforce for the first time

31 May–1 June 1916 Battle of Jutland in the North Sea

1 July 1916 Battle of the Somme begins

7 December 1916 Lloyd George becomes Prime Minister

1916 Coal is rationed, British Summer Time is introduced

1917 Food rationing is introduced (sugar, meat, margarine, butter, cheese)

15 March 1917 Russia's Tsar Nicholas II abdicates

6 April 1917 The USA enters the war

November 1917 Battle of Passchendaele ends; Battle of Cambrai sees first mass use of British tanks

11 December 1917 British troops enter Jerusalem, ending Turkish Ottoman rule

March 1918 Germans launch Spring Offensive

1 April 1918 Royal Air Force is created from Royal Flying Corps and Royal Naval Air Service

October 1918 German armies in retreat

11 November 1918 Armistice is agreed and guns fall silent at 11 a.m.

28 June 1919 The Treaty of Versailles officially ends the First World War

END OF AN ERA?

Was the pre-1914 world of the country house in Britain a 'golden age', as romantically remembered by some, or an illusion? The First World War cut short too many lives, ruined many more, and changed Britain's stately homes and British society. Wartime country houses and estates became part of a national war effort, and took on new roles – as military hospitals, convalescent homes, and centres for local agricultural, voluntary and charitable efforts.

After the First World War, commentators lamented the loss of a generation, and the high casualties among rich and aristocratic families who owned Britain's great houses and estates. Had the war, they asked, been the final blow to the old order? Indeed some estates had been feeling the strain long before 1914, but the war imposed new stresses, and the post-war world was unfamiliar, uncertain and sometimes unsympathetic.

Yet many grand houses survived, and evolved, some in new guises as commercially run stately homes with diversified activities and income-streams. A few continued as family homes, at least in part, while others passed into public keeping, preserved as landmarks in the heritage landscape and iconic reminders of a vanished world.

▼ *Pre-war elegance at the Duchess of Sutherland's garden party. Society hostess, reformer and author, the duchess had an eventful war: in France leading an ambulance unit in 1914, she was captured but escaped to run a Red Cross hospital.*

Before 1914, large country houses were symbols of wealth and success, hereditary and recent. Wildly varied architecturally, they still seemed to stand for stability; in them were represented Victorian values and Edwardian elegance, and such houses were an ideal setting for the extravagant seasonal networking of the well-connected. Almost every key figure in British imperial and economic life passed through these grand country houses. King Edward VII as Prince of Wales had made country house parties fashionable, and though George V lived more soberly than his father, the 'country house set' went on enjoying its pleasures, secure in the conviction that it still ran the country, and the Empire.

ON THE MOVE

Itinerant noble families moved between several large homes on the social round. The 9th Duke of Devonshire, his duchess and their seven children, began the year in Ireland, at Lismore. Children, nanny, governors, nursery maids, valet, ladies' maids, ponies and dogs were all packed into a special train to catch the boat across the Irish Sea. From Easter to June, the family was in London, with a Whitsuntide break at Chatsworth.

▲ *Lismore Castle, Co. Waterford. The Irish home of the Dukes of Devonshire is still in family ownership.*

BRITAIN BEFORE THE WAR

In 1911, the census revealed Britain's population to be just over 36 million. Of the 7.5 million private dwellings, the few thousand country houses had an influence and income out of all proportion to their number. About 90 per cent of Britain's children went to school from ages 5–11, but only 60 per cent were still at school at age 14. The sons of the gentry fared better: after school and the university (Oxford or Cambridge), most ran estates, went into the army or navy, or the Church. Daughters could be a problem. To have five daughters, commented Mary Harcourt, could be a terrible affliction, since their mother had to find 'five fools to marry them'.

... was seldom done before late at night. Coal for fires, water for baths, muddy clothes and boots to be cleaned: there were many back-breaking labours. Staff scurried between workrooms: boot room, pantry, scullery, coal store, still room, linen room, and so on. Separate 'routes' up and down stairs and along corridors ensured that food on the way from kitchen to dining room did not collide with laundry or chamberpots on their way down from the bedrooms.

◄ *Victorian bright buttons and starched linen: the domestic staff at Brayton Hall in Cumbria, about 1880. The house they served burned down in 1918.*

July found them in Eastbourne, then it was back to Chatsworth, before heading north to Bolton Abbey in Yorkshire for three to four weeks, followed by a month at Hardwick Hall, and back to Chatsworth for Christmas.

PARENTS AND CHILDREN

In aristocratic families, some parents and children met infrequently. Older boys were away at school. Girls were either at school, taught at home by a governess, or 'finished' abroad. Small children ate in the nursery under the watchful eye of a nanny who often clashed with the cook over the dietary requirements for her charges. Older children went downstairs for Sunday tea; otherwise family meals were the exception. A nurse usually slept in the same room as the youngest baby, and while older children had their own rooms, their rooms and the nursery often became a repository for worn furniture, as well as toys.

SLOW CHANGE

Electric light, telephones and motorcars were adopted by the 1890s, though cautiously. Large staffs were still needed, though antique house-cleaning techniques (damp goose wings to brush velvet, for instance) were giving way to vacuum cleaners. Although central heating and bathrooms with hot water on tap were now thought less 'foreign', most large houses remained decidedly chilly in winter.

While gentlemen ran their estates, or were in London running the country, ladies supervised the house and its domestic staff. Large country houses were major employers of labour, with servants indoors (butler, valet, footman, lady's maid, cook, 'tweenie' etc.) and outside (gardener, groom, poultryman, farm labourer, bailiff, gamekeeper, blacksmith and chauffeur among them). Estate carpenters made wooden doors, wheelbarrows and well covers, and repaired chairs, ladders, hen-houses and cold frames. Rural crafts such as coopering and basket-making survived on estate farms, and different counties still had distinctive styles for haystacks and even for bill hooks and scythes. The war was to erode the passage of traditional skills across the generations, and many rural crafts faded in the years after the First World War.

NEW MONEY

Conspicuous consumption by a fortunate few was squeezed by wartime restraint, including food rationing, but some upper-crust families had been feeling the pinch long before 1914. Wealth in the new 20th century was counted in cash, rather than acres, and vast estates did not guarantee vast incomes.

Some country gentlemen had expensive tastes: notably the Turf, but also hunting, shooting, foreign travel, steam yachts, gardens and (for some) exotic dancers and actresses. Many families with ancient titles and lands were obliged to shake hands with 'new money' – selling out to bankers, industrialists and merchants often anxious to acquire a noble home to match a recent title. Typical of estates in new hands were Luton Hoo (Sir Julius Wernher, diamonds), Crown Point in Norfolk (the Colemans, mustard), and Thornton Manor in Cheshire (Lord Leverhulme, soap).

Even as war clouds darkened, those prosperous enough to aspire to a country house browsed *Country Life* magazine (first published in 1897), and contemplated the architectural splendours of Edwin Lutyens and the garden designs of Gertrude Jekyll.

▲ *Castle Drogo, Devon, the 'last castle in England', designed by Edwin Lutyens for Home and Colonial Stores tycoon Julius Drewe. Work began in 1910.*

COUNTRY HOUSE PARTIES

Country weekends required high-powered organisation. At Blenheim Palace, the Duchess of Marlborough regularly invited 30 or more house-party guests, each bringing a maid or valet. The Marlboroughs drove from London on Saturday to check the rooms and menus, and decide on seating at table. Etiquette decreed that officers, diplomats and clergymen might sit down to lunch or dinner. Doctors and solicitors might take tea, but not often dine. The war brought more informality, deplored by some.

▼ *Blenheim Palace, Oxfordshire, gifted to the 1st Duke of Marlborough, and Winston Churchill's birthplace. The Palace library became a ward in the wartime military hospital, and Blenheim, like other houses, had to adapt as family and estate workers went off to war.*

▲ *Luton Hoo in Bedfordshire. Originally an 18th-century Robert Adam design, it had just been 'upgraded' for diamond merchant Sir Julius Wernher, and in wartime became an army convalescent home.*

Some aristocrats strapped for cash married money. Between 1900 and 1909, one in nine brides marrying noble landowners was non-British, and there were more than 50 American peeresses by 1914. American heiresses made seductive brides; in an 1899 'gilded marriage', Viscount Harcourt, roué and owner of the Nuneham Courtenay estate in Oxfordshire, wed Mary Burns, niece of US banker J. Pierpoint Morgan. The bride's emerald tiara was stupendous, and the 'Harcourt emeralds' were later worn at the 1937 and 1953 coronations.

servants. New money might commission new buildings, and shore up old houses, but by 1914 Britain was showing a few cracks. The war was to be a challenge not just for the country house, but for the nation as a whole.

As news broke of the shooting of Austrian Archduke Francis Ferdinand on 28 June 1914, the country house year was in full flow. Most house-party guests were less interested in central European politics than in the sporting and social highlights of the summer. The assassination of the Archduke seemed of passing interest only, until the rapid mobilisation of armies across Europe soon brought home the reality of what was unfolding.

A FINAL FLOURISH

Shortly before war came in 1914, architects were still busy designing country houses that were in many ways the last of their line. Late Edwardian houses included the Wittington Estate (1898) in High Wycombe, built by Reginald Blomfield for Hudson Kearley (later Lord Devonport), owner of International Stores. Another was the neo-Georgian Houndsell Place (Wadhurst in Sussex) designed by Alwyn Ball, an architect who was to be killed during the war.

New houses were easier to run than older mansions, crumblingly expensive and over-reliant upon

▲ *Hardwick Hall, Derbyshire. The soldier-heir to the Cavendish estates survived the war, to succeed his father and become 10th Duke of Devonshire in 1938. Hardwick Hall passed to the National Trust following the duke's death in 1950.*

THE LIGHTS GO OUT

THE CALM BEFORE THE STORM

August 1914 brought flower shows, harvest suppers and funfairs. Villagers in their Sunday best trooped up to 'the big house' to enjoy sideshows, listen to the village band, and gawp at the family's guests parading on the lawns: cool flowing dresses, hats and parasols, white jackets or blazers, Panama hats and canes. Ladies still changed dresses at least five times a day (morning, walking, afternoon, tea, dinner). There was cricket, croquet, tennis and badminton, and Polesden Lacy even had its own golf course.

Amid the tinkle of teacups and the supping of ale on such summer days, Europe's war, declared just before midnight on 4 August, seemed the faintest of distant rumbles, though Foreign Secretary Lord

▲ *Pre-war country pursuits: the Zetland Hunt in Yorkshire in 1911. Hunting, shooting and fishing were almost obligatory on some estates.*

▲ *When war came, people looked back with nostalgia on Edwardian tranquillity, with summer hats and tea on the lawn as here in 1906.*

flag-waving as volunteers flocked to join up in 1914, ill-equipped to fight a modern land war. Most officers from country house families, brought up with horses, longed to join the cavalry and looked forward to a short, dashing campaign, soon to be settled by a peace deal. Few people in Britain were clear as to what the cause of war was, and most were persuaded it would all be over by Christmas.

Grey memorably foresaw gathering gloom: 'the lights are going out all over Europe.' At home at Bedale in North Yorkshire, Dorothy Beresford-Peirse wrote of her reaction to the news, which was probably typical: the war seemed 'a rather distant thing … it didn't sink in.' Others felt a sense of foreboding, of an end to an era of calm. In Hampshire, Lady Laura Ridding confided in her diary that she felt 'shorn of the peace, in which all of our elderly lives have been wrapped'.

IMPERIAL TREMORS

Britain in 1914 was a nation still confident of its imperial might, but no longer as dominant as in the 1880s. The Royal Navy might rule the oceans with its battleships and cruisers, but Britain's traditional coal, iron and shipbuilding industries lagged behind innovative manufacturing and engineering in Germany and the United States.

Britain's army was small, and despite the enthusiastic

➤ *Kitchener's command drew volunteers from town and country to swell the army.*

London Opinion

"YOUR COUNTRY NEEDS YOU"

1ᴰ LONDON OPINION 1ᴰ

◀ *Kiplin Hall, Yorkshire. This 17th-century house survived the war to face new challenges.*

COUNTRY VOLUNTEERS

Volunteers 'taking the king's shilling' to join the army included estate workers, joining the thousands from industrial towns enlisting in 'pals' battalions'. The new soldiers were inspired and encouraged (even bullied) by their employers and landlords, some of whom formed their own military units. The patriotic fervour of 1914 drew on the tradition of local militias and the Territorial Force, formed in 1908 with a 50:50 split between cavalry and infantry units. Many country house squires and their sons were prominent as officers in county-based regiments, and allowed their grounds to be used for camps and training exercises.

▶ *Kiplin Hall gamekeeper Anthony Spence (33). He joined the Yorkshire Regiment in May 1916 and lived to tell the tale, coming home in October 1919.*

LOSSES MOUNT

The army expanded rapidly from August 1914, and even more so with the recruitment drive for Lord Kitchener's New Army in 1915. By then it was clear the war was not going to be short or dashing; casualties were already mounting. To cope with the appalling manpower losses on the Western Front, conscription for all men aged 18–41 was introduced during 1916.

THE DEFENCE OF THE REALM ACT

Country life was affected by new legislation in 1914, which allowed the military to take over land, and councils to seize unused fields for food production. Flagpoles were banned. Homing pigeon-owners needed permits. No feeding of bread to chickens or horses was allowed, nor was the ringing of church bells. No buying binoculars. Pubs had to shut early. Even the clocks changed, with the introduction in 1916 of British Summer Time.

After he answered the call to the colours, his mother went to Gloucester Cathedral to see him parade with his men before leaving for the front. Her youngest son Yvo joined the army straight from Eton; he was in France by September 1915, and dead a month later, aged 19. Hugo survived until April 1916, when he too was killed, aged 31.

▶ *Bridget Talbot, a cousin of Kiplin Hall's owner, served on the Austrian-Italian front, providing first aid and food for wounded Italian soldiers. She owned Kiplin from 1937 and campaigned to save the house and its contents, creating a charitable trust in 1968 to care for them.*

The bloody battles drained human resources from the country estates, and scythed down rich and poor alike, among them many fathers and sons of landowning families.

There were many sad stories. Hugo Charteris, Lord Elcho, son of the 11th Earl of Wemyss, and heir to estates in Gloucestershire and Scotland, was an officer in the Gloucestershire Yeomanry.

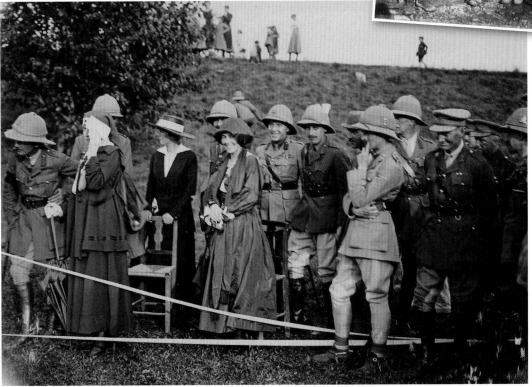

▲ *Bridget Talbot (centre, smiling) at a horse show behind the Italian-Austrian front line in September 1918. A reminder, perhaps, of a country house childhood.*

Country houses were expected to help the war effort by supplying land and accomodation (for hospitals and training), manpower (from their staff), and materials, especially food, livestock, and timber. The government was desperate to increase food production. Agriculture in Britain had been in depression since the 1870s, and landowners had begun to dispose of unwanted land, breaking up estates in some cases to sell off farms to tenant farmers. The war brought more adjustments in estate management, with older rural crafts superseded, and more machines; by 1918 there were fewer farmhorses and fewer farmworkers.

▲ Food rationing in 1917 produced the inevitable queues, illustrated in a wartime postcard with a popular soldiers' song.

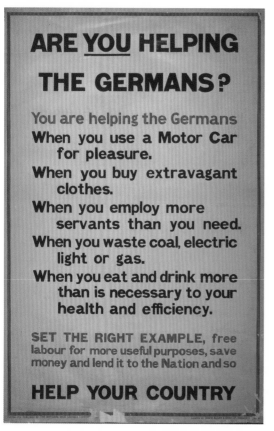

ARE **YOU** HELPING

THE GERMANS?

You are helping the Germans

When you use a Motor Car for pleasure.

When you buy extravagant clothes.

When you employ more servants than you need.

When you waste coal, electric light or gas.

When you eat and drink more than is necessary to your health and efficiency.

SET THE RIGHT EXAMPLE, free labour for more useful purposes, save money and lend it to the Nation and so

HELP YOUR COUNTRY

▲ 'Don't waste' appeals included this polite suggestion that genteel shabbiness could be patriotic.

OFF TO WAR

In 1914 many estate workers had skills of value to the army (they could shoot, use an axe or other tools, drive horses or motor vehicles). On the whole, they were healthier and stronger than town-bred recruits, about 40 per cent of whom proved to be medically unfit. Some landowners went to great lengths to encourage their employees to enlist. They promised estate workers that their jobs would be safe, with guaranteed incomes for their families while they were away. Volunteers were offered cash bonuses and rent-holidays as

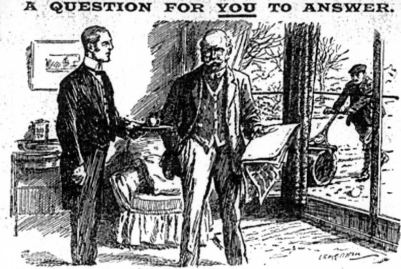

▶ *'Have you a butler, groom, chauffeur, gardener, or gamekeeper serving you who at this moment should be serving his King and Country?' asked this 1915 cartoon in* Country Life.

Have you a butler, groom, chauffeur, gardener, or gamekeeper serving you who at this moment should be serving his King and Country.

an inducement, and a few workers were even threatened with the sack if they did not join up.

New soldiers marched away bearing gifts of chocolate and tobacco, with the cheers of families and friends ringing in their ears. Men from the royal estate at Sandringham joined the 1/5th 'Sandringham Company' of the Norfolk Regiment. Most were killed at Gallipoli in August 1915. A memorial cross and tablet unveiled by the King and Queen in 1920 outside Sandringham church honours their memory.

THE FOOD DRIVE

In 1915–16 the Earl of Selborne, President of the Board of Agriculture, asked counties to set up local War Agricultural Committees. The government was anxious to increase wheat production, fearing bread shortages, and Selborne wondered about recruiting a 'ploughing and reaping corps', using men from the army. In 1916, with horrific casualties mounting on the Somme, this was a faint hope.

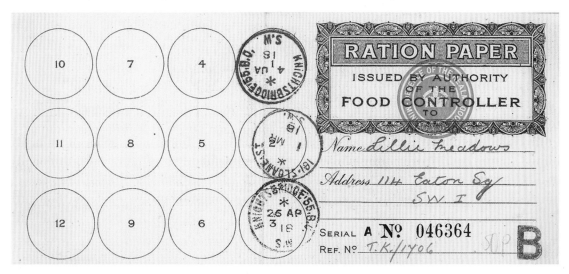

▲ *A ration sheet from 1918; rationing came when shipping losses caused fears of food shortages.*

WAR ON RABBITS

Edward Hudson, owner of *Country Life*, acquired Lindisfarne Castle on Holy Island, and from 1901 had it refurbished by Lutyens and Jekyll. In 1918, Hudson was upset to find Holy Island's gamekeeper trapping rabbits, arguing that as he rented the field in question, he also owned the rabbits. He was told that culling rabbits to protect crops was country custom, and the local War Agricultural Committee would not look kindly on the cultivation of rabbits.

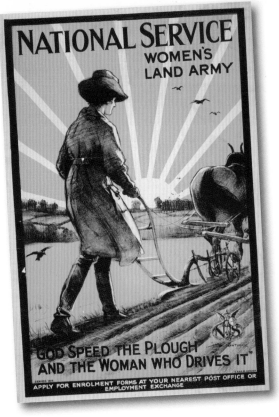

In the event, no one starved and not-too-stringent food rationing was delayed until 1918. However, everyone who owned farmland was urged to use it to its fullest potential, with local committees checking land was being farmed productively and vermin controlled. Fox hunting continued despite the shortage of men and horses in the shires (some cavalry officers rode to hounds on the Western Front), but shooting parties were less extravagant. King George V, a keen shot, had commented after a 1913 shoot that bagging 4,000 pheasants in a day was perhaps rather too much of a good thing.

⌃ *Ploughing a sunlit furrow. Uplifting posters invited women to join the Women's Land Army and head for the farms.*

An Illustrated War News *photograph of 'Women staffing an army remount depot' in June 1916.*

WOMEN DIG IN

Some women took the opportunity to get involved in agriculture and horticulture in a way not thought 'proper' before. Young women joined the Women's Land Army; their mothers the Women's Central Agricultural Committee, which told people how to garden more productively. Society ladies, such as the Marchioness of Londonderry, were prominent organizers; Lady Londonderry headed the Women's Volunteer Reserve whose members adopted military-style uniforms for tasks such as driving, first aid and running canteens for soldiers. The Women's Legion (1915) was less military-looking but also appealed to rich women used to running big houses (and telling other people what to do).

➤ *A humorous view of public concern at the risks of sending unchaperoned young women to work on the land.*

When Women **WORK** on the Land.

WOMEN'S LAND ARMY

The Women's Land Army went to work in 1917. At its head was Lady Gertrude ('Trudie') Denman, who ran Balcombe Place, a Sussex estate bought by her wealthy father. Not long back from Australia where her husband had been governor-general (1911–14), she had previously organised schemes to send cigarettes to soldiers, and save food scraps to feed chickens. Lady Denman raised an army of more than 250,000 women to work on farms, doing the work of men away at the front.

THE SCHOOL FOR LADY GARDENERS

Before the war, some country house women had sought independent lives. Frances Wolseley, only child of Field Marshal Wolseley, ran the School for Lady Gardeners at Glynde in Sussex. Her book *Gardening for Women* (1908) encouraged women into horticulture and market gardens, for both independence and national sustainability. During the war Frances, a viscountess after the death of her father in 1913, lived with her mother at Massetts Place near Lindfield.

THE SERVANT PROBLEM

Country houses needed a small army of servants. The 15th Earl of Derby, who died in 1893, had more than 700 staff! The 1901 census recorded 1.3 million workers as indoor domestics. Domestic and estate work was hard, the hours long and the pay modest, but 'going into service at the big house' could mean a job for life. Despite the rigours, it was less injurious than factory or farm work, and the tasks within the capabilities of most men and women, some of whom were by modern standards underfed, under-educated and physically frail.

▶ *Women took the wheel in growing numbers, Blenheim's lady chauffeur representing 'one of the many changes the call for men has brought about'.*

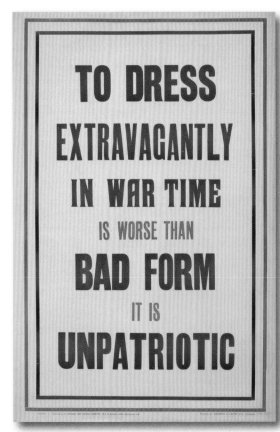

▲ *Hard times meant not just doing without a valet, but being exhorted to change once-fashionable ways.*

DOMESTIC RUMBLINGS

Yet by 1914, servants, especially young ones, were unwilling to drudge from 6 a.m. until 11 p.m. without complaint or more money. Change was afoot. *Mrs Beeton's Book of Household Management* in its 1915 edition noted the chauffeur as a new member of the domestic staff, though it largely ignored the war other than commenting that 'heavy taxation' was affecting country house life. The suggestion was made, however, that mistresses of great houses might learn to cook, at least a little.

House-owners were hard pressed to maintain traditionally large staffs. The war took away the able-bodied men, and young women left to find more interesting and better-paid work. Facing up to the 'servant problem' forced owners to consider alternatives. Some shut up most of the house for the war, and retreated to a few rooms – a drastic measure. Others studied helpful hints on 'making do', such as getting rid of old ornate

furniture and ornaments that needed too much dusting and polishing, and envied neighbours with 'modern' interior designs that were easier to maintain. The far-seeing bought vacuum cleaners and washing machines, though *Country Life* magazine declared in August 1914 that 'indulgence in luxury is not only a foolishness but a crime'.

Chatsworth, Derbyshire (above, today and below, before 1914) survived the wartime economies and manpower losses, to flourish into a new century.

LET THERE BE POWER

Electricity began to transform country living before the war. Pioneered by innovators like Lord Armstrong at Cragside, the world's first house lit by hydroelectricity, electric power was a boon to house-owners looking to modernise. They put in internal phones, to get rid of bells. They bought washing machines, electric mangles, ironing machines (with rollers), and 'hydro-extractors' (spin driers). Even so, laundering over 1,000 items a week remained a massive task.

THE COST OF AUSTERITY

At Goodwood, home of the Duke of Richmond, 20 house-servants in 1913 had dwindled to 12 in 1917, though this cut the duke's staff costs from almost £9,000 a year to just over £3,000. Dukes and duchesses, and others lower in the lordly scale, lamented the loss of valets, cooks, maids and, most of all, the butler, lynchpin of so many households. More expendable were gardeners and grooms; flower beds were allowed to deteriorate, while work was directed to the vegetable garden.

By 1917, Chatsworth's once-huge gardening staff was down to 20, the youngest aged 43, and Joseph Paxton's enormous Conservatory, which needed 10 men to run it, had to be left unheated because of coal shortages. All the hothouse plants perished and the Conservatory, the world's largest glasshouse when erected in 1841, was demolished in 1920.

DOMESTIC MICROCOSM

The 1911 census revealed the world of staff in a typical country house. At Hinchingbrooke in Huntingdon, the Earl of Sandwich employed a valet, cook, lady's maid, kitchen maid, scullery maid, and butler, plus a dozen other domestics aged 16–62, including carpenter, apprentice engineer and blacksmith. The gamekeeper and his wife had the keeper's lodge, while the 'motor cottage' was home to the chauffeur's family.

Horses had been an integral part of pre-war country house life, for work and pleasure. The war accelerated change. Fewer riding and carriage horses were stabled as grooms went away to saddle cavalry mounts and tend the thousands of horses and mules serving in the army hauling guns and wagons.

▲ *Cliveden House, in Berkshire. Waldorf and Nancy Astor turned the grounds into a Canadian army hospital.*

➤ *Canadian soldiers recuperating at Cliveden show locals how to hit home runs.*

DECLINE AND FALL?

It was inevitable that pre-war standards began to slip. Polished silver and a well-turned-out footman no longer seemed to matter to families grieving over lengthening casualty lists. As the months passed and battles came and went, newspapers, magazines and soldiers' letters gave hints of horrors, though censors screened out the appalling carnage on the battlefields. Wounded men back from the Western Front were reluctant to talk about their experiences. There was no television to bring instant, graphic war-reporting into people's homes, yet by 1916–17 most people had little doubt that the 'great war' was a catastrophe with profound implications. With revolution looming in Russia, some even began to wonder if the 'golden age' of the country house was gone for ever.

AIRSHIP OVERHEAD

The Home Front brought unexpected dangers. Although there was no fear of invasion (unlike in 1940) people in the south-east of England watched the skies fearfully for enemy airships. Air raids were a new threat. On 19 January 1915, the German Zeppelin airship *L45* dropped several bombs on the King's country house, Sandringham. One bomb crater was later turned into a duck pond.

War casualties hit almost every family with particularly high attrition among frontline army officers, who led men 'over the top', and were often the first to be mowed down by machine guns. Death shattered family hopes and plans: wives lost husbands; children, fathers; a son killed meant a reordering of inheritance; a fiancé lost often meant a lifetime of loneliness. Death was no stranger to family life before 1914 – childhood illnesses, infections and epidemics were all feared in an age before modern drugs and antibiotics – but the war reaped a grim harvest, scything through rich and poor.

> Rudyard Kipling penned patriotic appeals, but was hit hard by the loss of his son, killed in action in 1915.

THE LOST GENERATION

The bereaved usually maintained a dignified reserve appropriate to the upper-class code; public tears were not for the ruling classes – nor, it should be said, for the rest of the population, stoicism being a British characteristic in 1914–18.

People bore their burdens of sorrow in private, often continuing with public activities in mourning black. To the wives, mothers and sisters of the fallen, commanding officers wrote letters of condolence, invariably lauding the dead man's comradely virtues and courage, and adding that he had been proud to

▼ Kipling's Sussex home Bateman's was, he said when he bought it in 1902, 'unfaked' (no bathroom, no electricity). It became a retreat and his home until he died in 1936.

FLOWERS TO THE SCYTHE

By Christmas 1914, 95 sons of peers had already been reported killed in action. The war brought many more personal tragedies. Edward Hardinge, son of the Viceroy of India, died of wounds received in 1914, which meant his younger brother Alexander became 2nd Baron Hardinge of Penhurst on the death of their father. Rudyard Kipling lost his only son killed at Loos in 1915, and at his Sussex country house, Bateman's, the writer farmed to aid the war effort, with Mrs Kipling as dairymaid.

die for his country. To soften the blow, most letters of condolence informed the family that death had been 'instant'. Those left to carry on remembered the dead and honoured their sacrifice, but patriotic pride could not soften the blows to so many households.

C.F.G Masterman, in his book *England After the War* (1922), felt the war had decimated a generation, for 'in the retreat from Mons and the first battle of Ypres perished the flower of the British aristocracy'. The consequences seemed plain in post-war Britain; every day the newspapers carried notices of sales, 'of estates running into thousands of acres'. This gloomy picture of death-toll in the shires coloured many recollections of the First World War as the death-knell for the old social order and country house families. This became a popular theme in post-war fiction, featuring elderly estate-owners, bereft of sons and grandsons killed at the Somme or Ypres or Loos or Passchendaele, struggling to keep up appearances, shivering with cold in winter, watching gardens turn into weed-tangled wildernesses, and selling off the family silver.

THE FINAL BLOW

What often happened was that the war applied the *coup de grace* to estates already in financial trouble, the weakest collapsing under tax burdens intensified by death duties. When the Duke of Devonshire died in 1908, his estate was liable to £500,000 in death duties: a Shakespeare folio had to be sold. Estates with less valuable assets were hit hard by wartime higher rates of income tax and rising interest rates, which bit those already bleeding from debts and mortgages.

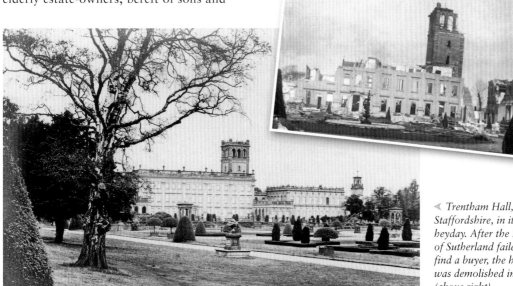

◄ *Trentham Hall, Staffordshire, in its heyday. After the Duke of Sutherland failed to find a buyer, the house was demolished in 1912 (above right).*

▲ *Longleat, Wiltshire, which became a Relief Hospital during the First World War. The Marquess of Bath's son and heir, Viscount Weymouth, was killed in 1916.*

Hard-up estates faced the same fate as houses that had fallen before 1914, such as Trentham Hall in Staffordshire (see p.21). Once among the finest houses and gardens in England, Trentham was offered in 1910 by its owner, the Duke of Sutherland, to Stoke on Trent city council. The council declined to buy, so the house was demolished.

To cut costs, and to cope with shortages of fuel and staff, some owners moved out altogether, to hotels. Visitors to Lord and Lady Grey found them dining in the housekeeper's room, while Lady Howick, her house turned into a military hospital, persuaded convalescent soldiers to stand in as chauffeurs and gardeners.

SELLING OFF

Weakened by years of depressed farm prices, estates that had struggled through the war were hit in 1919 by increased death duties (charged at 40 per cent on estates over £2 million). The result was a post-war flood of sales. In 1920 the Duke of Rutland sold off half his Belvoir estate for £1.5 million, while the Duke of Sutherland released over 250,000 acres of land in Scotland. The 6th Duke of Portland, owner of more than a dozen residences before the war, had by the 1930s cut them to four.

Estates dependent on agricultural income were exposed, without the financial cushion of London

DEATH DUTIES

There were few millionaires in pre-First World War Britain (between 1880 and 1909 only 22 estates were valued at over £2 million). Death duties were introduced in 1898. When the Duke of Westminster died in 1899, death duties of £600,000 (roughly two years' ducal income), were met by selling off property in London. Wartime death duties struck hardest those families where a son and heir was killed soon after his father had died – a double hit. By 1918 some estates were paying up to 80 per cent of their rental income in taxes and maintenance.

property, coal mines, or factories. So they sold farms, often to tenants already in possession. In 1914 only 11 per cent of farmland in England and Wales was owned by its occupiers; by 1927 this figure had risen to 36 per cent. 'England is changing hands' claimed *The Times* in 1920, and by the end of 1921 the *Estates Gazette* estimated that a quarter of the country had passed into new ownership. To some observers this represented the biggest transfer of land in England since the Dissolution of the Monasteries in the 1500s, possibly since the Norman Conquest.

➤ *Eaton Hall convalescents during the First World War, relaxing in pre-war country house style.*

▼ *Eaton Hall, Cheshire, about 1894 when rebuilt by Alfred Waterhouse (the Natural History Museum's architect). With 150 bedrooms, such grandeur could not last. Demolition came in 1961.*

HOSPITALS AND COMFORTS

Many great houses were turned into military hospitals and convalescent homes. The lady of the manor often made herself 'commandant', though an army quartermaster saw to food and other supplies, and a professionally trained matron ran the wards and supervised the nurses, many of them young women volunteers from the Voluntary Aid Detachment (VAD).

BACK TO BLIGHTY

Faced with a torrent of casualties, army medics on the Western Front made life-and-death decisions every day: who to try to save, who to send home, who to relinquish to death. Those soldiers sent back to 'Blighty' (Britain) were the lucky ones, having escaped the most serious wounds and survived post-wound infection and trauma. They included men declared medically unfit through 'shell-shock', fatigue and debilitating illnesses,

▲ *Rest and recuperation in a very English manner: Nurses vs Patients at Isleworth military hospital (Percy House, formerly a school).*

◄ *An enviable nurse-to-patient ratio is apparent in this relaxed scene, posed at the Relief Hospital at Longleat in Wiltshire.*

► *At Woburn Abbey, the redoubtable Mary Russell, Duchess of Bedford, ran the military hospital.*

including tuberculosis and venereal diseases (for which special hospitals were set up). The most seriously wounded cases were treated in specialist hospitals, eventually, perhaps after a series of operations, joining convalescent homes. Many of the wounded were prescribed massage and physiotherapy to ease pain and restore mobility.

NURSED BACK TO HEALTH

Country house hospitals were recovery centres for thousands of soldiers, some of them officers who in peacetime had been guests in those same houses. Noble ladies turned fashionable London town houses into hospitals and convalescent homes, where officers might enjoy a club-like atmosphere with all the comforts including fine wines and gossip. Country house hospitals offered spacious accommodation, fresh air, regular meals and calming landscapes: respite and recovery for battle-damaged minds and bodies after the shell-blasted nightmares of the front.

Among the military hospitals was Woburn Abbey. Here the Duchess of Bedford, a trained nurse, turned the riding school and indoor tennis court into a medical facility staffed by nurses, with estate workers as ward orderlies and stretcher-bearers. The duchess worked 16-hour days, in the operating theatre and at her desk. Others were equally busy. The Countess of Selborne took charge of the hospital at her Hampshire home, Blackmoor House (now flats). The drawing, dining and smoking rooms were wards; the hall a living room for the men, the library a sitting room for nurses, and the billiards room became a store room. In Yorkshire, Lady Beresford-Peirse ran Bedale, the family house converted to a 20-bed convalescent home, insisting that her daughter Dorothy not be 'exposed' to casualties (other than take wounded soldiers for drives in the pony cart). In 1915 Dorothy, then 21, moved to Harewood House (see p.27), also a convalescent home, although the earl was still in residence, to help his daughter who was looking after the patients – under the practised eye of a matron.

Many young women were enthusiastic volunteers. Vera Brittain, who left Cambridge University to become a VAD nurse, found even dusting 'inspiring', though the glamorous Diana Manners (later Lady Diana Cooper) raised eyebrows by changing her nursing dress for an evening gown and disappearing to late-night parties.

REST AND RECUPERATION

At Highclere Castle, West Berkshire, Almina Countess of Carnarvon sought financial help from her father, the banker Alfred de Rothschild, to buy the most up-to-date medical equipment and provide a staff of 30 nurses, a medical director (the family's doctor), and to convert a bedroom into an operating theatre. Highclere, the setting for the television series *Downton Abbey*, was ideal as a war hospital; for the Earl and Countess of Carnarvon, it was rather like having a permanent house party, with wounded soldiers as guests, and with the house staffed on pre-war levels for its wartime role.

House-hospital owners provided comfort and entertainment of a familiar and usually decorous

▶ *The Royal Pavilion, Brighton, in 1894. Queen Victoria had rather liked 'this strange building', which became perhaps the most eccentric-looking army hospital during the First World War.*

▼ *Indian soldiers were presumably thought to feel more at home surrounded by the ornate Oriental décor of the Dome Indian Hospital at the Brighton Pavilion, 1915.*

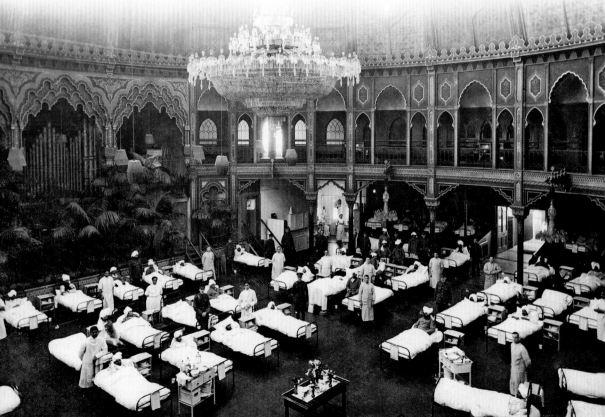

REFUGEES

Some large houses took in refugees, most of whom came to Britain from Belgium – about 100,000 Belgians had fled from the advancing German armies by the end of 1914. The Countess of Carlisle, a campaigner for temperance and women's rights, provided cottages to house 150 refugees. There were more than 2,000 refugee committees across Britain, helping to settle people from Belgium.

nature. Social distinctions were invariably observed. Officers felt at home; 'other ranks', sometimes confused with staff, perhaps less so. When not fussing around their charges, the 'ladies of the manor' were busy organising charitable activities: village sewing and knitting parties, first-aid classes, and fund-raising sales to send chocolate, cigarettes, warm socks and other goodies to soldiers at the front.

Few army hospitals looked more imposing than Harewood House, near Leeds, where Dorothy Beresford-Peirse of Bedale nursed soldiers.

FAMILY FORTUNES

The 1914–18 war is often seen as a watershed in British history. For many social commentators post-war, Britain's decline, even in victory, seemed to be symbolised by the decline of so many landed estates, and the loss of a generation. The nostalgic view is of Edwardian ebullience and confidence transformed into decay and uncertainty, with so many families grieving for their losses, and country squires mouldering in crumbling houses they could no longer afford to keep up.

DIVERSIFY TO SURVIVE

Some house-sites have seen a succession of changes, all radical. Drakelowe Hall in Derbyshire, home of the Gresleys, was demolished in the 1930s; in the 1950s the site was used for a power station, now also gone; and its modern incarnation is as a village-development.

As the victory celebrations of 1918 and the 'Roaring Twenties' gave way to slump of the 1930s, many estates managed not only to survive but to diversify. Very large estates such as the Duchy of Cornwall's, and those of the Dukes of Atholl, Buccleuch, Northumberland and Westminster, grew and thrived after the First World War. The largest, spread over several counties, already had varied interests: the Duke of Northumberland, for instance, got 40 per cent of his income from coal mines (amounting to £73,000 in 1914). Other owners had substantial and profitable property holding. The Grosvenor, Cadogan and Portman estates drew income from London rents; the Derby

RESTORING THE PAST

The Society for the Protection of Ancient Buildings (SPAB), founded by William Morris, Philip Webb and others in 1877, sought to protect old houses and castles from 'restorers'. Much was 'restored', like Hever Castle, taken over by J.J. Astor in 1919 when he returned from the army, and Bodiam Castle, secured by Lord Curzon during the war. After the war, Gordon Selfridge dreamed of building the world's biggest castle (250 guest suites) on Hengistbury Head in Dorset, but architect Philip Tilden's scheme got no further than a plaster model.

▼ *Clumber Park, Nottinghamshire, survived the 1914–18 war, but only just, after a fire in 1912. Built for the Dukes of Newcastle but far too large and costly, the house was demolished in 1938.*

▶ *Hever Castle in Kent, where J. J. Astor, decorated for bravery in the war, succeeded his father as owner in 1919.*

and Sefton families had properties in Liverpool; the Scarbroughs in Skegness; the Devonshires in Eastbourne; the Norfolks in Sheffield, and so on.

Some landowners followed a trend already begun before 1914, to downsize: they emulated the Duke of Newcastle, who in 1908 had given up his Nottinghamshire home at Clumber Park, and moved to a smaller residence near Windsor. Clumber Park survived the 1914–18 war but the house was demolished in 1938 – the parkland survives. Some noblemen felt they were doing the right thing socially and politically by selling, citing the example of the Duke of Bedford who in 1909 sold part of his Thorney Abbey estate in Cambridgeshire to his tenant farmers, as a liberal gesture.

SELLING UP

Sales were rarely driven by crushing taxation. Of 40 noble families who sold land in 1916, only six had recently incurred death duties. Some owners decided they no longer wanted to live like their forefathers, and packed up and left; others saw that modernisation and rationalisation made economic sense. A boom in land sales between 1918 and 1924 saw the Dukes of Beaufort, Northumberland and Rutland, as well as the Marquess of Bath, all dispose of chunks of estate land. Tenant farmers were usually keen to buy their farms, since farmland had become more valuable during the war. The 1917 Corn Production Act, guaranteeing grain prices, was a short-lived boost to landowners, though the grain boom ended with the repeal of the Act in 1921.

A NEW WORLD

Country houses that in some cases had been in the same ownership for 300 years or more, emerged from the 1914–18 war into an uncertain new world. Some entered somewhat inglorious chapters in their histories: Chiswick House, an 18th-century jewel that had become a mental hospital in the 1890s, was sold in 1929 by the Duke of Devonshire to the local council; during the Second World War it was used as a fire station. It is now restored to echo its former elegance.

In the 1920s and 1930s, forward-looking and well-managed estates survived thanks to economies, cash injections from rents and sales of city properties, and eased tax burdens (in 1930 estates were allowed to become limited companies).

And for a while the upper-class social round continued on its traditional merry way. The 1914–18 war relaxed certain social conventions, but long after it ended some traditional rituals continued, such as young ladies 'coming out' and being presented at Court. Families with social aspirations still sent their daughters to London for the 'season' of balls and parties, shopping and social calls, their chaperones keeping a watchful eye open for prospective, and suitable, husbands. The season flickered on through the Second World War, into the 1950s.

EPITAPHS AND REMEMBRANCES

Victory in 1918 was greeted with parades and parties, but amid the relief and rejoicing was a deep sense of sorrow and unease. Memorials testified to the losses in every community – including many great estates, such as Castle Howard in Yorkshire, where memorials commemorated the latest casualties among generations that had fought in battles from Waterloo to the Somme. Remembrance Day, first marked at the Cenotaph in London in 1921, became a solemn national commemoration of all those, from bootboy and gardener to butler and baronet, who had marched away, never to return.

The 1920s flickered with promise of prosperity, but 1929 brought the Crash and the 1930s the Depression. By the time the Second World War began in 1939, many country houses had been sold for redevelopment, or turned to new uses. Some, like Bryanston in Dorset, a house designed in the 1890s by Richard Norman Shaw for Lord Portman, became schools or other institutions. Perhaps as many as 1,000 large country houses were 'lost' between 1900 and the 1950s.

PUBLIC PROPERTIES

The National Trust was founded by Robert Hunter, Octavia Hill and Canon Rawnsley in 1895 to preserve landscapes rather than houses, but after 1918 Lord Lothian, owner of Blickling Hall in Norfolk, was prominent in urging the Trust to help preserve country houses, and estate villages too. The government was pressed to exempt historic houses from death duties. Castles too were in need of public protection: Bodiam Castle was gifted to the Trust in 1925. A further National Trust Act in 1937 enabled owners to transfer a house and contents to the Trust to maintain tax-free, and after the Second World War (1939–45) there was a steady flow of properties to the Trust, including Blickling, left by Lord Lothian to the nation in 1940. English Heritage, set up in 1983 as a successor body to the Ministry of Works, similarly cares for a number of historic properties, as do Historic Scotland and Cadw, in Wales.

▼ *Castle Howard in North Yorkshire. Like many great houses, its estates included several villages, and the war impacted on families rich and poor across a community.*

SURVIVORS

Whether in family, public or corporate management, the great country houses of the British Isles remain landmarks in local and national life. Through exhibitions, performances and by being open to visitors, they serve as gateways to the past, as well as being places so many enjoy visiting.

Estates with houses at their hearts are often vital components of regional life, with varied business activities. Every year they offer millions of visitors a glimpse into a world shaken but not destroyed by the war of 1914–18, a world often far removed in character from our own. Grand houses appeal to the imagination, with their rich personal stories and aesthetic and historic legacies. Having survived two world wars in the 20th century, they seem well-placed to survive the 21st century too.

➤ *Coneysthorpe war memorial, in the village close to Castle Howard, includes the name of Lieutenant Michael Howard (a son of the 9th Earl and Countess of Carlisle). He was missing, presumed killed in action, at the Battle of Passchendaele in 1917.*

PLACES TO VISIT

BATEMAN'S
Bateman's Lane, Burwash, East Sussex,
TN19 7DS; 01435 882302;
www.nationaltrust.org.uk/batemans

BLENHEIM PALACE
Woodstock, Oxfordshire, OX20 1PP;
01993 810 530; www.blenheimpalace.com

BLICKLING ESTATE
Blickling, Aylsham, Norfolk, NR11 6NF
01263 738030 www.nationaltrust.org.uk/
blickling-estate

CASTLE DROGO
Drewsteignton, Near Exeter, Devon,
EX6 6PB; 01647 433306;
www.nationaltrust.org.uk/castle-drogo

CASTLE HOWARD
Yorkshire YO60 7DA; 01653 648333;
www.castlehoward.co.uk

CHATSWORTH
Bakewell, Derbyshire, DE45 1PP; 01246 565300;
www.chatsworth.org

CHISWICK HOUSE
Burlington Lane, Chiswick, London, W4 2RP;
020 8995 0508; www.english-heritage.org.uk/
daysout/properties/chiswick-house/

CLIVEDEN HOUSE
Taplow, Berkshire, England, SL6 0JF;
01628 668561; www.clivedenhouse.co.uk

GOODWOOD HOUSE
Goodwood Estate, Chichester, West Sussex,
PO18 0PX; 01243 755000; www.goodwood.co.uk

HARDWICK HALL
Doe Lea, Chesterfield, Derbyshire,
S44 5QJ; 01246 850430;
www.nationaltrust.org.uk/hardwick

HAREWOOD HOUSE
Harewood, Leeds, LS17 9LG; 0113 218 1010;
www.harewood.org

HEVER CASTLE
Hever, Near Edenbridge, Kent, TN8 7NG;
01732 865224; www.hevercastle.co.uk

HIGHCLERE CASTLE
Highclere Park, Newbury, RG20 9RN;
01635 253204; www.highclerecastle.co.uk/

IGHTHAM MOTE
Mote Road, Ivy Hatch, Sevenoaks, Kent,
TN15 0NT; 01732 810378;
www.nationaltrust.org.uk/ightham-mote

KIPLIN HALL
Near Scorton, Richmond, North Yorkshire,
DL10 6AT; 01748 818178;
www.kiplinhall.co.uk/contact

KNOLE
Sevenoaks, Kent, TN15 0RP;
01732 462100;
www.nationaltrust.org.uk/knole

LISMORE CASTLE
Lismore, County Waterford, Ireland;
+353 (0)58 54424; www.lismorecastle.com

LONGLEAT HOUSE
Longleat, Warminster, Wiltshire, BA12 7NW;
01985 844400; www.longleat.co.uk

LUTON HOO Hotel, Golf & Spa,
The Mansion House, Luton, Bedfordshire,
LU1 3TQ; 01582 698888;
www.lutonhoo.co.uk

ROYAL PAVILION
4/5 Pavilion Buildings, Brighton,
BN1 1EE; 03000 290900;
www.brighton-hove-rpml.org.uk/RoyalPavilion